Home Green Home

A Declaration of Love for Ireland

by
Eduard Schmidt-Zorner

Home Green Home

A Declaration of Love for Ireland

by Eduard Schmidt-Zorner

Southern
Arizona
Press

Southern Arizona Press
Sierra Vista, Arizona

Home Green Home

By Eduard Schmidt-Zorner

First Edition

Author: Eduard Schmidt-Zorner
Editor: Paul Gilliland
Formatting: Southern Arizona Press
Cover Artwork: Eduard Schmidt-Zorner

Published by Southern Arizona Press
Sierra Vista, Arizona 85635
www.SouthernArizonaPress.com

ISBN: 978-1-960038-29-6

Poetry

To my wife Marian, a Kerrywoman

Reviews

I have long admired the writing of the multi-lingual, multi-talented Eduard Schmidt-Zorner, or as I know him under his penname, Éadbhard McGowan. His work is wonderfully lyrical and descriptive, having within it the capacity to convey the reader to far-flung places, ancient landscapes, and unfamiliar experiences. Nowhere are his skills more evident than when taking us on a tour of his beloved adoptive country, Ireland.

Home Green Home begins with an account of his unpromising arrival on Irish shores. Soon however he is at home as he takes us to the heart of this ancient land, *Caragh Lake*, where we '*...feel the pulse of time*'.

Page by page, the poet explores his new surroundings, flitting at will between the real world and the world of dreams, filling our senses with the tastes and sounds of this new/old land. When he dares to stray, Ireland draws him swiftly back, to Kerry, to *Caragh Lake* and to that most mystical place, *Ard-na-Sidhe*, the Height of the Fairies, where one of their number '*...gathers moments in a wicker basket/to feed dream fish*'.
Fishermen too fill his pages, find comparison with their compatriots in ancient Galilee. Ravens and cormorants inhabit the rocky shore.

We move inland to ancient bogs, redolent with history. *Fuil Cheilteach* – Celtic Blood – and Celtic mystery in every line. Here, and in the pages that follow, Éadbhard displays an outstanding grasp of our culture and traditions.

As a native Irishman myself, I find it almost unbelievable that he wasn't born and reared in Ireland. As my old grandmother would have said, *He's been here before!*

John McGrath – Fellow Kerry Poet, Lisselton, County Kerry / Ireland

Hi Eduard,

I really liked your poetry. You have a great talent for words and creating evocative scenes in one's mind and memory. I liked your bit of Irish in *Bray Head* also!

Poem on *Caragh Lake* also brought back memories of fishing there years ago with my husband and the gorgeous scenery and wildlife all around us on the lake.

I felt the same as you about cities in *Outlook of a Traveller,* whenever I am in a city, especially at night when I can't even see the stars in the sky, I want to escape immediately back to the hills of Kerry too!!!

Thank you for sharing some of your thought provoking and memory provoking poems with me and hopefully I will see them published in Ireland soon.

Bernie O'Keeffe – Artist from Kilbeg, County Mayo / Ireland

Eduard is known for writing stories and poetry in many languages. We are fortunate this talented multi-linguist has shared, in our own language, his contemplations of his life experiences and friendships across the globe. Through his words and images, one's senses are filled with the tastes, sounds, and sights of 'other'. No matter where you're from, you will be sure to appreciate this collection.

Pamela Muller – Artist and writer from Kenmare, County Kerry / Ireland

Contents

Foreword

Dear readers,

I am honoured to present to you this collection of Irish poems, inspired by the rich culture, history, and landscapes of this beautiful country that has welcomed me with open arms. As an immigrant to Ireland, and an Irish citizen by now, I have been humbled by the warmth and hospitality of the Irish people, who have made me feel like one of their own.

Love brought me to Ireland; my wife is a Kerrywoman. Therefore, I have a double reason to be grateful.

Through this collection, I hope to express my deep admiration and gratitude towards Ireland, its people, and its traditions. These poems are my love declaration to this land that has captured my heart and soul.

Ireland, Mother Ireland, thank you for embracing me and inspiring me to write these verses.

I hope that my poems kindle in you the same feelings and convey the same love and appreciation that I feel for Ireland, that they offer a glimpse into the beauty and magic that makes Ireland so special and that my poems will resonate with many readers, whether they are of Irish descent, have visited Ireland, or simply appreciate the art of poetry.

May these poems evoke positive emotions in you, and may they serve as a tribute to the timeless charm of this enchanting country.

So here's to you, dear Ireland,
My love for you will never end,
For in my heart, you'll always stay,
My home green home, every day.

Eduard Schmidt-Zorner

Two Mothers

When my mother died,
I lost my childhood.
When I left the motherland,
I lost my identity,
my language, my words...
my nationhood.

An orphan, abandoned...
I looked for shelter, desperately,
crying loud on empty streets.
In my hometown
waiting for the train to the airport,
to another land.

I left a reed on my mother's grave,
a last wave.
A child left alone.
Nobody there to care.
I arrived on another shore.
A stranger, not heartedly accepted;
no banners with *Cead Mile Failte*.

An old woman came up to me,
Mother Ireland,
Grey haired, with a big bosom.
She nourished a lot of children.
Clasping me to her chest,
she said: "You are my child"
I was saved, accepted.

Caragh Lake

A rock in the lake,
a withered pine on its shore,
we bring the boat to water,
and sink into silent lore.

You like to cut reed,
to prepare a bed.
Wind blows over the grass.
Herb scent is our bath.

The crickets fall silent,
the sun reflecting in the water.
A heron walks with a saunter,
splashing in shallow waves.

The evening casts a shadow
over the yellow fields,
tired by the midday sun.
Around - steep heathered slopes.

Reddened sky on the horizon
colouring the dripping oars.
We moor, feel the pulse of the time.
The moon will soon appear.

Bray Head

I climbed up the mountainside,
it's almost like a way to heaven,
solid ground beneath my feet,
clouds are within reach,
flowering broom hides a wren,
seagulls over slopes and *glen*.

By the wayside stood a cabin,
stretching over the horizon
like a loaf of soda bread.
Fuchsias spread their flowers
over the garden's fence.

A front garden, overgrown.
I reflect on the wild roses.
A woman opens her door,
throws a questioning glance,
her fiery red hair flows.

I asked her: "*Conas atá tú, ar maidin?*"
She kept silent, not a word,
and I said: "*Tá an gruaighe go háilinn.*"

She shook her head,
like a wave was her hair,
surging like sea water
through the morning air.

Days later I walked the path again
to admire the roses and her hair.
No house to be seen.
A field full of fern and butterbur.
A dream it must have been.

Eduard Schmidt-Zorner

Cork from One to Four

Grand Parade,
where ships moored formerly
taxis are now quay-siding.
Venice *Éireann* sank into marshland
or between house shores and bridges,
island between converging channels,
open to seafaring.

Crubeens, tripe and *drisheen*, a treat,
are mouth-watering and mingle
with varying degrees of rhoticity.*
One should not speak while eating!
Corked ears, but the Word is whispered into them
at *St. Augustine's Church, Washington Street*.

The English Market offers temptations
and dead fisheyes,
triggering memories of the Queen's visit,
the French cheese, though, remained unimpressed.
Spices, promising images of faraway countries,
while housewives drag shopping bags.

Tuckey Street:
Where Freemasons meet.
Hiding their secrets;
I know them all by heart.
The door at No 1 opens for 2 seconds,
after 3 knocks,
a man in a black suit enters.

St. Anne Shandon chimes 4 times.
The salmon on the tower is
looking westwards to *Sneem*
to greet his brother,
the only two in Ireland
hovering over church spires. **
It is time to proceed to *Kent station.*

*Rhoticity
Accents of English can be either rhotic or non-rhotic. A rhotic accent
generally has /r/ more or less whenever it appears in the spelling. Many Irish
accents are non-rhotic but none of them could be described as upper-class -
much of north/central Dublin, Louth, the border counties, West Cork/Kerry
all have accents where the word-final R is omitted, and some don't even
rhotacise at the beginnings of words.

** There are only two churches in Ireland with a salmon as weather vane: St
Anne Shandon and the Church of Ireland in Sneem

Time for a Poem in Dublin

He is a famous street poet of the 60s
and still alive, he did not dive,
wears still the scarf around his neck
in a mischievous way
and has a look like *Steinbeck.*

I asked him if he ever read *Baudelaire:*
frozen real solid got he
wouldn't answer me.

He goes through a book,
photographs of poets mostly.
He is not in there.
He began too late and lived too long
in small rooms drinking whiskey
and avoiding the landlady.

I am no *Camus* but it bothers me to see
the halfwits making hay
out of tragicomedy, says he.
There is only one place
ALONE with a typewriter or a keyboard.
Because the writers of the street
get their soul sucked out by idiots.
They all want to kill your creativity.

The poem is carefully typed, not an error.
Double-spaced the words.
It's a horrible one, it speaks of the terror
and some tragedy
in the 19th century.

Outlook of a Traveler

When I saw the steel-grey scarring sea in *Aberdeen*
in front of me,
behind me the cold grandeur of the granite city...
I felt that I had to flee
back to the hills of Kerry.

When I saw the pulsating, anonymous *London,*
with boiling traffic driving a strong surf against me...
I felt I had to escape from this dungeon
to the hills of Kerry.

When I saw the repulsive architecture in *Frankfurt*
the suffocating towers of money,
suffered from the hurting noise of flyovers
and urban motorways.
I felt I had to escape
to the hills of Kerry.

When I saw the overcrowded narrowness of *Dublin*
and the misery on the streets...
I felt I had to run
to *Heuston Station*,
to get back to the hills of *Kerry.*

Cosan na Naomh

When the last tunes from the fair field
vanished into the evening air,
got caught on the church roof on a slate
protruding from the corner
and fell on the square.

When the merchants counted their yield
and the last showman moved on,
when all are gone
and gypsy Kathleen's
view in the future got blurred,
tool sellers gathered up their tools,
the carousels stopped rotating
and the drinkers debating...

I felt relieved.
We had enough show and illusion
we need substantiation.

Standing in front of St. James,
I remembered a recent book I read
about *Santiago de Compostela*
with a glass of *Rioja* in the hand
and the thoughts I had
dripping into my insomnia.

Just around the corner
our pilgrimage way starts
not under a field of stars in the high
or the great cathedrals
but under the Western sky.

Around the corner
peeped the God Lug
wagging his finger,
-at his side the *puck*,
water in a jug,
he left with a shrug,
a black crow cried.

I put on my boots
checked the new routes
took the staff
went around the bend
on the way of the saints.

A Moonlight Night

Strange, the darkness,
strange, the forest,
strange the rock at *Ard-na-Sidhe*,
on which the fascinating moon casts silver coins
to wake up a flustered fairy,
who gathers moments in a wicker basket
to feed dream fish
in *Caragh Lake*.

English Market

Loud talk, inside the market hall.
Smells, steam, and dust.
The merchant's stalls, the rust
of vessels.
People rush past fish counters.

Well matured cheeses in display,
remembering the makers hand,
when washed, salted, and turned,
then stored away in shelves,
left to mature quite naturally
to give *haut-gout*
to join the cider from Normandy
with the wine from Burgundy.

God dined in Ireland and lived in Brittany.

Dublin Awakes

In cosy darkness
the pub seems to be asleep
I glance through the window.
A flickering bulb
shines on a tired waitress.

A knock at the door
makes her aware of the early guest
A second knock is not in jest.

Pub front – inheritance,
tradition invites intuition.
A crow's cry;
a sound that will never
come back again.

The door opens,
The smell of a fry
brings memories back
of yesterday.

Rossbeigh

I walk on the beach
touch the sand with my feet
and cast a shadow on the dune.
Hardly recognize yourself anymore.
How you have changed
since last time
when I visited you?

You are not sedentary,
You are a dune.
Let yourself be carried away.
Sometimes the sea kisses you
in front of a whey-coloured sky.

There is no postcard with your picture.

Eduard Schmidt-Zorner

Nightwalkers

Kenmare bay rests calmly,
repeating waves drench my shoes.
The moon sees his reflection in the water
Is delighted.
You can see his happiness.
He shines unremunerated, out of friendship.
I owe him thanks.
Resting on a round stone I wait for the tide.
I am looking for hardly noticed creatures.
To perceive them, one has to be of the sea,
an eye on the receding water
with rolled-up trousers or unclothed.

Are they not sedentary?
On the stones and rocks by day
the *limpets* walk at night.
Residents of the intertidal zone,
neither high waves
nor rain or sun
can cause them harm
due to their adaptability.
You think, they are not *sessile*,
meeting them at daylight at the same spot.
During the night they wander,
as a mermaid suddenly finding legs to run away.
They are all on the move in the night.
Grazing algae lawns.

A Crow

At the *"Butler's Arms"*
I heard a pecking.
Was it on the windowpane?
Insane,
I thought,
looked up at the ceiling
where the sound echoed from...
And dust fell down
to dot my face with freckles.

Sun and Shadow

There is a chapel in a field
overgrown with brambles and weeds
on the river *Laune* for centuries.
Why did I force open the door
being told about the curse,
a secret to be guarded
about a face, the face of the head?
Climbed up *Lower Bridge Street*,
felt a sensation on the back of my hand,
drops of blood roll down.
Suddenly a rainbow stretches over the hill.
Invisibly behind me
somebody whispered into my ear:
"Let the Templars rest on top of the hill,
the encampment of old,
they fled a traitorous king, *Philippe Le Bel*
and *Clement V*, the Pope,
both died terribly."
"Let them rest.
The day of revenge will come
the blood line is still unbroken.
Watch the place: desecrated,
profane, defiled, to *Dionysus*
or *Bacchus* now dedicated,
what an abomination...
We will come back again
to take what belonged to
us. Final redemption."

Perspective

View of the mountains,
hidden behind hedges,
which, through a gap,
permits a glance,
revealing their beauty,
blocked by a gate
that looks like tally marks
in a prison cell:
vertical stroke, stroke, stroke, and slash.
In front, in the lush green grass
a dandelion.
Yellow flecking,
promising hope.

Paradise

Often wondered what
paradise looks like
or what paradise signifies,
what meaning it has for us.
A reward for good deeds,
for a life free of sins?
To be loved by God or Allah
or to sink into eternal Nirvana?
To have made a pilgrimage,
cared for lepers, the underprivileged,
to have been there for mankind?
Or just kept the mouth shut?
When I stand near *Doonreaghan*
and look over the Atlantic,
into the wide expanse,
see the curved horizon,
admire the glistening sea,
the peaks of submarine mountains,
which stretch into the ocean,
and spot the *Skelligs,*
inhale the scent of wildflowers,
listen to the birdsong,
the hovering flight of the gulls.
This is paradise.

Cromane

A feather tumbles from the sky,
iridescent green, brown,
with a white stripe.

A greeting from a goose
that took its flight,
so blithely light and spry
over the beach of *An Cromán*
fly, fly high, over fields,
the purple heather slopes,
the mountain pastures yields.

Eduard Schmidt-Zorner

Following an Irish Saying

A bit of your soul is trapped
in everything you crochet.
Knit in, a hidden fault,
so, your soul can escape.

Entangled in a network,
caught in the web
of your life construct
of fail and debt.

Studying yarn labels
without getting a sense,
wrap the yarn,
pull the loop.

Different colours,
patterns and stitches,
changing knitting patterns.
Everything is still hidden
in the ball of wool,
all possibilities are open.
Still at the beginning,
the thread is unrolled,
not torn or cut off,
stitch by stitch
neatly strings together.

The counting of mashes,
one right, one left.
The needles are rattling
in the rhythm of past seconds.
The hours, days, weave silently.

Soon a result, a whole is visible,
to be soon unravelled,
or to give moths a home.
Even the fault is no longer visible.

Ireland in 2034

They ask me once
to have a look into the future,
and paint an accurate picture
of coming events;
and I bluntly refused.

How can **I**, when forecasts,
prospective prognoses,
predictions, estimations
FAILED,
see, what lies in front of us
and succumb to speculations?

I am not Macbeth's Banquo
who was asking the witches
to speak a prophecy to him:
„If you can look into the seeds of time,
And say which grain will grow
and which will not,
Speak then to me..."

The seeds of time,
how would we know
how they will grow?
Seeds are we, the people,
we are the grains,
which grow,
prosper and decay.

There is the mighty MAY or MIGHT
many a night,
many a night will pass
and water under the bridge
will flow
how do we know
in which direction
our fate will grow?

The past reminds us
of predictions which never came
to a desired fame:
Thousand-year-Reich's lasted
twelve years, governments passed,
children died, who had a bright future,
careers ended, people were evicted,
tsunamis, earthquakes, volcano eruptions
all unpredicted.
Tomorrow a meteorite could hit the earth
or in about one million years,
and all life is finished.

To speak for my poor Ireland:
It might be lost to rising ocean levels
or be united, or more suppressed
by loyalists.
No flights, no cars, due to the
climate hype, a Marxist *Taoiseach*.
The Irish punt reintroduced;
the stag of *Killarney* seen
on the one *punt* coin again;
the Great Southern Hotel
for the homeless.
In the distance heavy shooting.
Uprise, food shortage.
Farmers protect their land
against theft and looting
by the hungry.

The last ones of a ruined society
try to reach a nearby planet
to cowardly escape,
condemned to stay on earth
which they so effectively destroyed.

Puck

Summer is announcing its end.
Days get shorter now
after Puck, they say.
Farmers save the last hay.
Lonely nights get longer.

The goat had a photo shooting
on a field in *Dromavally*.
The pagan feast is cancelled.
God Lug had no power either
to free us from the plague.

Hope that the days, though,
would not get shorter, vanished,
it crept in unnoticed
and utter reality teaches us
that the rhythm is maintained.

We slip into an uncertain autumn
without the soothing consolation
of bright warm summer days,
with the dire prospect that
next year still will no puck fair be.

Intaglio

The mountains
which I see from my window
were given a name.
They have a sequel
like a serial novel,
and continue into the sea
to protrude,
and show their peaks
like the back of a reptile.
Memories of millions of years remain,
between the earth's crust
and thin cloud cover,
peaks, point to the West,
to the curved horizon,
into the wide Atlantic.
From my window
I can see the clouds
that stand over *Kenmare,*
on the other side of the ridge,
which divides the *Iveragh Peninsula,*
and I think of the house
where aunt Lilly lived,
who always told stories
in her distinctive dialect.

From the window I see the hedges
that border the fields,
in a different shade of green,
and some spots of white and black
move very slowly ahead,
sheep and cows graze
and above them
crows, magpies, and gulls,
each with their own right to exist,
like visitors that came from afar
and soon disappear,
safety returns and peace for a wren.
I see what the ice age has left us,
the slopes shine in the sunlight,
cloud shadows mix colour into dark green.
The fields,
wrested from the steep mountainsides,
form geometric patterns,
squares and rectangles,
like a book with open pages.

Eduard Schmidt-Zorner

An Cromán

A friendly wave from a man
who works in the fish factory.
They have put three on the spit.
One at the start,
the second in between,
the third at the end,
to keep a distance
as if in quarantine
far away
from the built-up land.

But there is only the smell of seaweed
and the iodine of the sea.
Trawlers lie on the water - three
and a few boats.
On a truck
grow-out mesh bags
and steel rebar racks.

A tractor leads a boat to water,
a fisherman jumps in,
starts the motor
on a cold windy day
at the 'hip bone'
where the sunrays fall
on the incoming tide.

Fishermen in their yellow jackets
throw out their nets
and seagulls glide over them
to see if something is left
to feed their constant hunger.

The spit has its toes in the Atlantic
and beds prepared for the mussels.
Fishermen, weather-beaten men,
in tune with nature,
with the salty water,
hardworking
like those in *Galilee*
who brought in the catch
on a stormy day.

Sea Ravens Near Fenit

I take the boat along the coast,
visit the habitat of cormorants
on their rugged island,
their fortress-like outpost,
opposite the port of *Fenit,*
where yachts bob on the water
in friendly unison,
dreaming of a sailing holiday -
St. Brendan overlooks the bay.

On the coastline nestle villages,
a settlement protrudes, green fields.
Sounds emerge from homesteads,
hammering, noise of tractors,
cattle raise their heads.
One can see *Bolteens*
and I remember the pint
which I drank there
where opposite a horse
got new shoes at a farrier's.

On the water the sun glistens,
the island in the distance
stretches the head out of the sea.
On top perch the big sea ravens,
obviously sociable birds.
Now and then one of them rises,
dashes down, disappears in the sea,
comes back to the top, dripping,
sometimes with
or without prey in the beak,
holding their wings out in the sun
to dry their dark feathers.

Over the blue-grey sea
an elongated band of clouds.
I approach the cormorant colony,
let the boat drift, without paddle.
The sun sends golden rays,
the wide surface ripples,
where tongues of wind descend.
A spell of calm, makes the water
shine and smooth like a mirror.

The shore out of sight,
land seems far away.
Me, between grey sky
and steel-grey infinity.
Lonely seagulls fly.
A tranquil mood ascends
after the cry of a sea sprite
or was it a mermaid
who sang her song, so light,
so ethereal, so weird?

Fish swarm under the surface,
in a water deep and dark.
I approach the protruding rock.
The cormorants are startled,
make noise in their nests,
warn the rest of the flock.
A lively flapping of wings.
They escape into the air,
swoop, and dive away.

Irish Full Moon

I see you in the dark firmament
like a sallow lantern,
over the *MacGillycuddy's Reeks*,
your bright round face
gives me joy and peace.
You do not make me blink
or dazzle me,
a planet mild and pale
in a sea of black ink,
makes its way across the sky,
strides along, silent and shy.

I would like to paint you green
to match the landscape,
copy for you the sheen
of these fresh slopes, the fields,
all the emerald shades
that here exist,
then release you over the peaks
or let you sink behind them
so that after your journey
you rise again
above the mountains
and cast a silver shine
upon them.

Eduard Schmidt-Zorner

Kennedy's Cross

I often drive past
an abandoned shop
near *Callanafersy*,
as I did recently
on my way to buy bread
in *Milltown*, or vegetables,
or visit the graveyard
the last rest of relatives,
or via *Castlemaine*
and beyond to *Tralee*
over the mountains,
where the Celtic Milesians
defeated the *Tuatha de Danann*,
and *Scotia*, who died in battle.

So again, last week
on my daily drive,
I ask myself:
is the owner still alive?
I pass again
the corner shop
at Kennedy's cross,
as it is called,
where the road branches off
at the *Tinnahally* road
near the N70.

There might be
no direct connection,
there are so many Kennedys
in this nation.
But it reminds me,
it triggers memories
of a great president.
I think of this man.
So brave, so Irish,
so clear a vision,
remember him with awe
he saved the world
from a nuclear war.

Fuil Cheilteach

Evening walk across the bog,
breathing in eternity,
caressed by *máthair* nature
cradled in her maternity.
At the horizon in the West
the sun descends
behind the terrestrial curvature.

Bare feet touch the ground,
where cutters have dug the peat,
uncovered vivid mysteries,
with each turn of the *sleán*,
layer by layer, unfolding centuries,
treasured in dark brown, heavy,
sacred wetland.

Sundown over boggy ground,
sombre, resilient, profound,
the wanderer's rest,
a transition from our sober world
to the unfathomable' Otherworld.'
The sun disappears, goes to bed.
There is only her red shine left.

Under ancient peat layers,
they found the adorned corpse
of a king, sacrificed for the gods,
with his *torc*, the golden ring
around his neck,
remnants of the Celts
proving pride and strength.

Ancestors' whispered words
come from the mainland,
from their old Gaelic land,
boundaries that *Caesar* exemplified:
'*Gallia est omnis divisa in partes tres..*'
It wakes hidden memories,
make the blood throb and boil.

Returning to the Celtic realm,
to its mysticism, its secrets,
which were hidden, buried, forgotten,
as if under a deep-water surface.
I am like a swimmer, striving
towards the light, towards the air
to discover the shrouded past.

A pagan prayer sent
to the goddess *Andraste*
to tempt fortune, to fathom fate
by the course of the running hare.
Consume hand-chosen sloe fruits
to fall into a dream or trance,
and look into the past.

Chronicle of time immemorial,
blood line disembogues in the present.
One cannot escape fate.
Red flowing life stream,
of persistence and resistance,
of Celtic fury
and, finally, survival.

Crann Bethadh

I have many roots,
am widely interlaced.
My branched roots
are like the mushroom spawn,
the fine mycelium.

I derive from two trees.
Their roots grow deep,
root deep in the ground,
fan out to all sides,
fertilized by the dust
of Celtic tribes,
drenched with Celtic blood.

Searched for, found,
in Europe's East and West,
in ancient Celtic lands,
it took a balancing act
from Thuringia
to *Aix-la-Chapelle*.
Just wondering
why there is this distant calling
from far, of Celtic sounds,
in my heart resounding -
So wondrous.

Mystic trees,
their shoots are used for grafting,
for pruning a tree
that now stands tall in *Eire*,
finally.
I stand here, proud,
my roots anchored in the earth
Eternally. Immovable,
monolithic.
Celtic.

Part I now am
of this tree of life,
whose branches reach high
into the heavens,
its roots dig deep
into the Earth
all are interwoven,
the connection
between Heavens and the Earth,
rooted in *Uisneach*,
the centre of the land.

Trees are spiritual,
mystical beings,
not inanimate objects,
a source of great wisdom,
with the power to bridge
the gap
between us and the Otherworld,
representing Mother Earth's bounty
and the eternal seasons' cycle.

Eduard Schmidt-Zorner

Home, Sweet Home

As we descend,
we break through the clouds
and I see the patchwork of green fields,
caressed by the evening sun.

In my heart, my burning love for this land,
the hedgerows, the gently grazing cattle,
sheep, like cotton dots
on the lush pastureland,
the dear mountains in the background,
in a haze.

You have me back again
and I have you.
Even creativity is coming back,
inspiration nourished
by peace and calm,
a soul balm.

Back home, sweet home.

Summer Threshold

The morning comes with tangy air,
pulls bushes and trees out of the mist.
In the windbreak of the timber forest
deer fray the velvet from their antlers.
From the green sedge, the trunks shine red.

Jays make a noise in the thickening,
overgrown moor forests host brazen crows,
wanderlust of the grey geese,
lapwings stagger over the swamp meadows,
worried for their young, with plaintive cries.

Hidden in the reed bed of the riverbank,
a grey heron stands.
Lonely on one leg and contemplates.
From the nearby rye field,
the illusion of the smell of bread,
the air sings, and the earth listens.

No hunter's shot.
All is full of lust -
a summer without end.
The first heavy raindrops fall on my hand.

August Evensong

Eventide's breeze flows soft-winged.
A woodlark sings.
Sunshine spreads on undulating hills,
dew-wind unites with winding rills.

Wafts from the sirens' song
oscillate like sounds of the sea,
deep subconscious longing
gives us time to think.

Crickets fiddle in the grass,
a creek runs through rough stones,
the rose glows in the garden,
gorse blooms along the fields.

From far, a jackdaw's scream,
then a long and heavy sigh,
as if the mountain takes a breath,
gusts are falling from high.

Buzzing through the treetops
see a swarm of rushing birds,
hear from the beech slope
the wingbeats of a dove.

Shepherd and flock seek rest
near fields of corn abundance,
in orchard's ripened apples
still rests the summer silence.

On sylvan peaceful scene
the sun is shining brightly,
and stripes of light lightly
turn the glade into a sundial.

The late summer's sun
rests on bare rock's face
to grant to moss and ivy
a last warm favor's grace.

Waiting for the reaping hook,
rich meadows' golden gift,
soon yet the austere, rough
threshers' work comes to an end.

Harvest celebrations fade
around the rich filled barns,
on the farmhouse's threshing floor
summer night drapes veils galore.

The opulent harvest time
is gone, the green pollen waves
and dust of rye and wheat fields
are blown and flown away.

Scurrying through fences' laths,
from the stable to the shed
slips a marten's fleeting shadow
swiftly up the birch tree's trunk.

From deep forests soothing silence,
when the silent star balls glow,
distant monotone night's song
of steady falling waterfalls.

Final strokes of nine
peal from a village tower,
the whining of a mandolin
over the dreaming hover.

Hay Moon's Morn and Eve

Mellow are the July nights,
when the sunset's reddish fading
and the early morning lights
dawning blur and blend.

When summer with red roses
bleeds to death so rapidly,
cawing ravens mourn the dead,
the blackbird has not sung
its last song yet.

Warm rays from the sunset
make distant peaks glow red,
the scream of the wild eagle
sounds over the forest silhouette,
while pale-cold falls the mist
into the closing day.

Under lime trees, under elms,
under thatched roof's hanging wings
overgrown with moss and weeds,
stretching wide and shielding.

I want to put it into a song
what on the moonlit village green
I heard the fairies lisping.
What grey stone's mossy green
inscription said to me.

Fog pictures rise in the twilight,
from the dark days 'past.
I hear faint voices whispering,
sounds of pleasure, lament, anger.
A last farewell, so distant.

Silent night in the deep forest
around the birches' black-white bark;
around the alder's trunks so dark,
flows the moonlight soft and mild.

Green Shall Remain the Earth

When the evening casts its grey net,
on the horizon
a strip of solemn pine appears.
The day sinks, the sun extinguishes,
as if it never existed.

Raptors' cries above the treetops resound,
the wide rye fields wave abound,
rooftops visible behind woodland,
rural silence floats to the rising stars
to mark the warm day's end.

Lost, remain the swampy lakeshores
around the boggy resilient grounds,
with reeds and tall sedge
at motionless water ponds.
An owl screams in the thicket,
a crake fills the clearing with its call.

Last dying rays over the slope
like a trinket.
The yew tree shields the graves
of Celtic cemeteries,
a dove coos,
sound of murmur in the sacred grove.

The hair, anointed with olive oil,
lush the mint, the laurel adorns the head.
Darkgreen ivy hangs on the wall
in competition with wild wine and roses
the cypress stretches tall
I offer fragrant posies.

Unexpected

I bath my feet in the water
of a mountain stream,
who speaks gnome-like to me,
chatters and mumbles incessantly.
Willows hang their branches
into the foamy water,
as if surrendering,
powerless, sad, and tired.

Toads begin to spawn.
Butterflies tumble high.
The wailing cry of a buzzard in the sky.
The bark of a fox,
and hark,
a dog's responding bark -
Then a leaden silence,
like under a hood, a glass dome.

A quiet, so soundless.
Motionless.
Suddenly, a crackle, a breaking.

An old oak branch,
like a grey-brown snake,
crashes onto the path,
hits the ground with a dull sound -
the call of a pheasant hen.

Then it is quiet again.

Snow Moon

Wind from the north-west
grooms the wild lyme grass.
We observe the sky,
contemplate the moon's shine,
enjoy the crickets' choir,
they sing into the night.
To prevent a fall
your hand rests in mine.

Forest Myth

The forest, familiarity confers,
holds many lives in disguise.
It is still wintertime, freeze.
Ice and snow transform trees
into bizarre shapes.

Soon, a mild wind wakes
the forest from wintry slumber.
Lively forest abode:
In the basement a pack of wild boars,
in the cellar a fox's den,
in the attic the wood grouse
with its black gown.

Spring moss, filigree sporophore,
scatters millions of spores.
In March, hazelnut blossoms,
open their pollen grain,
generate pollen rain,
subtle explosions.

Cones of conifers
send their seeds
on an uncertain journey.
Love-play in the wind,
pollen dust, gold stain.

Symphony of colours,
shapes and smells,
anemones attract insects
with their seductive scent.

Wild garlic promises taste,
indulgence, a stimulant.
Light controls the process,
warm are the sun's rays.

Bright day events change
with nightly shadow signs,
accentuated strange noises.

Thunderstorms are brewing,
rain is heavily pouring.
A toad runs away, puzzled,
a leaf on which a beetle sits,
is hit by a drop
the beetle flung away.

Then calmness settles.
Water evaporates,
steam clouds form
over the dense green.
Rich, fertile, odorous.

Farewell Letters

Tempus fugit, as the Latin says,
"time flies" the vernacular repeats,
as a trickle through a sieve,
unstoppable as long as we live,
irretrievable it escapes.

I do not see time as running out,
more likely to evaporate,
its farewell note is light and airy,
spring is passing, greenish as a veil,
a thin cloth, a gentle waft,
covered with pollen, powdered
with flower dust.

Summer finds it harder to say *adieu*,
lies heavy on us like a hot sheet,
resists, refuses transiency
with opulence, bearing fruit,
it shows maturity.
Amid life,
we are embraced by death.
Summer is not ready to accept
the last rose,
the last breath.

Autumn makes it easier to say 'goodbye'.
Just as the falling floatleaves
are the rain of many letters,
and pages of a book,
where everything is written down,
like calendar sheets with aphorisms,
and bygone dates.

Winter leaves its farewell letter behind,
puts it on the table,
for everyone to see, to read.
Cold is the fire of the fireplace,
corpse-cold,
a plume of blue smoke rises,
bare of words the writing is,
everything has already been said
with frost, snow, and torpor,
the vanishing white,
the emerging black.
Grey is the envelope.

Eduard Schmidt-Zorner

Oileán na Marbh
Island of the Dead

Hopes buried
under the grey stone
of a lump of rocky ground
on a beach in *Donegal*.
Grief and sorrow,
made the lips dry
of those who mourned,
their hearts torn
days full of doom
and gloom.

Tears do not dry in eyes
fixed on the boundary walls
near the unconsecrated ground,
that echo lamentation cries,
dry throats from prayers,
from harsh reality,
the island's sad history.

The dead little souls
carried to the island
in a small wooden box
across the beach at low tide
during the cover of night.

Powerless, no chance to grow.
Unbaptized, not their fault.
Famine victims, a genocide.
Birth outside of marriage,
all kept as a secret,
hoping nobody would find out.
Though spring was in the balmy air
a glare of frost set on the souls.
Like hoarfrost sticking to the wounds
where it stayed, and never went away.

Reoccurring images
come to our mind
when we walk in *Cromane*
or at the *Bay of Kells,*
see the childrens' graves,
the names of whom unknown.
Of people who committed suicide,
unknown sailors who died at sea,
or unrepentant criminals
were also buried here.

* Oileán na Marbh, resting ground for over 500 babies, a very secret burial ground

Eduard Schmidt-Zorner

Balancing Act

I love walking the bog
in autumn,
experience the mysticism,
the rising mists,
which settle like a frosted filter
on meadows, plains, and pastures.

Shy cranes, thousands,
start from their night camps
into surrounding fields
under a bright purple sky.
Now they move south,
silence returns.
Let us call it a break.
The roebucks chase the deer,
mark their territory.
The caterpillars cocoon
until next year.

The rhythm is always the same.
The sundew sucks out its prey.
Carnivorous.
The fox kills the lamb,
the buzzard the mouse,
the spider waits in the web.
I see a dead bird,
a crow in agony.
The farmers protect their bales
with poisonous grains.

A world in miniature.
Blossoms, live, wither away,
digestion, decay,
eat and be eaten.
An obscure, meaningless,
sad cycle.
Depressing, actually.

Maybe I will blot it out and enjoy,
intoxicate me with harmony,
will not criticize the nature of survival
at the expense of others
as a misconception of creation,
though it strangles my breath,
suffocates me.

The cheeping of the deer,
the snake lurks,
the crocodile waits,
just like Britain's nuclear waste
in the North- and Irish Sea
is about to disintegrate
and dissolve.

Waste in the oceans,
garbage dumped in Africa.
Glyphosate sprayed without need.
Bee death, insect death,
followed by human death....

Eduard Schmidt-Zorner

Conjecture on a Water Plant

Reed bent by a breeze,
a thinking reed,
thinking so deep
riverbanks so steep,
streamlets gush,
bluish-green rush,
bulrush,
bluerush, blue so blush,
fields so lush, full of hay.
At first blush - a silent day,
quiet cozy bowers,
pouring rain showers
hush little thrush!
Lizards hide
under sun-heated stone crush
at the wayside
greenblack, attentive, plush.

We pick fruits in
orchards, in the garden,
we harvest the wine
in wicker baskets
to keep the grapes.
We sort the apples,
sort pears and beans
we brush, clean the yard,
the leaves away.

The cooper seals with rushes
barrels full of grape blood
which splashes in goblets,
casks.
A bath in the lake to refresh.
Wood sedge, reed, and rush.

Ducks in their habitat dabble.
High in the sky,
an eagle eyes its prey
in the reedbed,
but it escapes.
An otter dares its way through the cane.
Autumn day closes its gates.

Eduard Schmidt-Zorner

Strawberry Moon

I look up from my book of poetry
and see your 'seek and hide' play.
You peek through the *Reeks'* valley
then rise like a released balloon,
let loose over the mountain range
on this night in June
and pour a silver glow
over the slopes and a lonely grange.

You are so close to us now
on your elliptical path.
So peaceful, so feminine, *Luna.*
Not like your wild brother *Sol.*
So round and full,
filling the sleeper's dreams.
Moving the ocean waves,
silently rocking the world
casting gentle shadows.

Weather Forecast

The weather gives us concern
it gives us grief,
especially when dismal
bores us when we see no clouds
that we can count.

Let us hear the concert of the wind,
the organ sounds of pounding storms.
Puzzling, cryptic, enigmatic.
Colours itself with red sunset
is changeable, often magical,
characterized by mood swings,
an eternal topic of conversation,
harmless, unoffending.

I wanted to become a cloud pusher,
paid by piecework.

Hope

The bow of the ship named '*Dóchas*'
rests on rockers and cradles.
The slides are lashed onto the deck.
Slowly stern-first the ship moves,
begins to pick up speed,
slides down the launchway
into the waves,
down the slipway
tilts to the left slightly,
then to the right,
it floats by itself proudly,
after enveloping the shipyard
in a fine-grained mist.
The ship turns and sails gently,
sends a loud blast
on its way
towards the setting sun
in the West.

Yes, something still has a future.

Ocean Rage

The storm, northsea-ish,
shakes up the sheets
of sleeping, now awaking dunes.
The seagulls hide
the sheep take shelter
in groomed marram grass,
or in a corner by the dike.
No one else to see.
Just gray foaming spray.
The lighthouse light extinguishes.
A steel-colored wall remains.
The ocean roars,
and howls through the night and day.
The spring tide comes.
What menacingly surges
against the shore
scatters salt into old wounds.

Eduard Schmidt-Zorner

Encounters on a Journey

In the airport
a woman from *Listowel,*
waits for her boyfriend from *Berlin.*
She knows people I know,
small world we are in.
She admires my writing of poetry
and we speak about the *Seanchai.*
The Moroccan intercity waiter
praises my Arabic pronunciation
and we rave about *Constantine.*
The Russian taxi driver,
glad not to be blamed for Putin,
encourages me to brush up my Russian.
I discuss with a Turkish lady the books
by *Orhan Pamuk*
and advise her to write
and we include the *Bosporus* in our talk.
Thanked a Kosovarian restaurant owner
who gave me food and water
when I felt weak when I passed by
last time
No charge.
"That is my culture", he said.

A Kashubian lady friend
hugs me for a long while.
Big town, melting pot, kaleidoscope.
Me, coming back to my past, as stranger,
meeting strangers in their present,
we all feel marginal.

But we unite,
a new culture emerges,
warm hearts, appreciative souls,
something to offer mankind.
I have a laugh with my neighbours
we exchange news, learn about
new events,
recent deaths.

Birds migrate and return for a while.
People migrate. Or choose the exile
and emigrate, take on a new identity
but we all share the same sun,
the gentle moon light, the air.

Diversity

When several cultures
have licked over your face,
practically one per weekday
and your tongue
gets around a few idioms,
one for every day of the week,
confusion takes hold
and you ask yourself
where do I belong to?

When you have two passports
and you contemplate
which one you like more,
my decision is easily made:
One took my love for granted
frustrated, disappointed me,
the other I fell in love with
a love that was instantly returned
Do you see my dilemma?

When you are at home in many abodes,
when the tongue,
well-versed in different sounds,
can differentiate between different foods
and voice subtle preferences,
and, you, incidentally, stop briefly by
in *Casablanca, Canton, and Nancy,*
where they share bread and rice with you
prepare groats or fish,
and, with a double espresso,
give it the final touch.

When you roam in the morning,
online,
through international media,
be it *Le Monde, NY-Times,*
Die Zeit, or *El País,*
your head might spin
with all the news
and the smell of their towns rise,
imaginary, into the nose of
a world citizen.

Eduard Schmidt-Zorner

Exuberance

No, it is not the ocean,
awaking my emotion,
not the flotsam, washed ashore
from the continental drift,
nor the waves, which always go too far,
or not far enough, adrift.

Certainly not the squawking seagulls,
the cormorants off *Fenit*
or the eagles.
Not the marine luminescence,
when, finally, the night falls
and answers the day calls,
not the grains of sand could be counted.
Spare me the sea urchins, cuttle-bones
on broken stones.
No algae or seaweed, no fish, no oyster ship
at *Cromane*, called 'the Hip',
only a dead deer and a broken fish box
smashed on the grey rocks.

Not the loneliness
and not a freshly washed tomorrow
thrown on the sand, no shattered boats
and torn nets found on the strand.
I flee the offshore wind,
leaving the lighthouse behind.

No legends please, leave me alone
with mermaids and sea sprites,
no salt on the skin, no salt foam,
no birth of Venus ...
but the endless expanse of the oceans
evokes my emotions,
the moon creates the tides and our dreams,
gravity miraculously keeps a mass of water
in a spherical shape,
eternity the tidal stream on this round planet,
until one day it atomizes into the universe,
when the earth ends.

Peeling the Spud

I must admit,
when I landed here,
in Ireland,
arrived at the green shore,
I held the potato in contempt,
paid little attention to it.
It was more of an addition,
support or base
for finer, more sophisticated dishes,
kind of giving undue volume
or as they later said:
a satiating supplement.

My mind, however, changed:
The cook had a potato face.
More precisely:
The beauty of the potato
was shining in her face.
Not only the bulbousness of it,
also, her skin as a whole
had that earthy glow
and shimmer of tangible happiness,
that lies matt on stored tatties.

Instead of potato,
she used the term 'spud'.
To be kissed by her meant
to be kissed by the sandy dry soil,
which was not an ephemeral,
but a saturating one,
like potatoes in their jacket
fill our stomachs.

She added,
except for sparingly rapeseed oil,
on Sunday melted butter,
during the week she converted the rest
into *champ* and *colcannon*
not to forget the bacon.
Sometimes green onions were added.
Or served with a humble cabbage soup,
to which beef bones gave a taste
and made grease drops swim
on top.

Or fried potatoes with lard,
mashed spuds with mashed apples
called 'heaven and earth'
with a bit of cinnamon.
Unsurpassed,
her jacket potatoes
with curd and caraway,
black pudding or brawn part of it,
of course, also potato dumplings.

My task was to prepare
the turbot and the brill,
stewed in white wine,
seasoned with capers,
to be blanketed in jelly,
wrapped up in sauces
and served on rural porcelain.

Wild goose baked in a clay coat
or roast rabbit with garlic,
goose giblets with chestnuts,
codfish sprinkled with dill.
All crowned with steaming potatoes.
The discussion about
flowery and waxy consistency.

I finally dared to take a chance
on this golden tuber myself.
A mystical undertaking.
Foaming salt and misty steam
in a stainless-steel old fashion pot.
The singing melody of hot water
when it starts bubbling.
In wise foresight:
nutmeg and caraway,
at my side,
chervil and parsley
all served
with a dollop of mayonnaise.

Songs were composed
to glorify the potatoes,
celebrating their versatility.
My ode, however,
is more powerful.

Transience

Write your name on the stone,
and throw it into the sea.
Or take a shell and scoop water,
wash away the word,
written in the sand.

Dry wood, flotsam,
a dead seagull,
a small wreck, the masts broken,
a dream shattered,
the word unspoken.

Eerie silence all around us.

My Poem for a Poet
Matt Hodd from Kerry

Written after we all assembled for the planting of his tree and some of his ashes were put at the roots of an arbutus:

Your ashes were put at the roots of trees
transferring energy, creativity, and memories;
returned to nature, to the eternal circle,
under the twittering of birds.

Matter decays, energy remains
For us, among us, between us.
The tree, element of regeneration,
concept of creation
between birth and death,
human collective work on earth.

Every man is creative, hence free.
Freedom and creativity make him see.
Transforming social organisms
into works of art,
reaching the heart,
that what you did, to reach
and open our hearts
through *Poetry in the Park.*

You now can say:
I am a tree, with epidermis,
clothed in bark,
my leaves show printed thesis,
my roots are in the earth,
the branches like an ark,
humus...constant rebirth.

Organic cycle of matter, fermentation.
In harmony with nature, transformation.
Key to happiness and beauty
the path of inspiration.
Let nature decorate the walls
and open our souls. Let algae rule.
May mould take over, fern, mosses,
and lichens
in the infinite intuitive fullness.

We, my poet brother, give you back to earth,
to nature, a nature you adored
and which you now
embrace forever.

Eduard Schmidt-Zorner

This Summer

Subtly, May passes into June
like morning passes into noon.
Without a breeze, trees rustle
as they did before.
No bustle anymore.

Dawn takes a deep breath.
Time slowly forebodes death,
dominated by utter silence.

The light adopts the colour
of freshly dyed silk,
soaked meadows the shade
of liquid green bottle glass
flowing down a hill.

Sounds are trapped
like air in a balloon,
silence weighs down on hope.
Doom.
Only an ominous chime of a bell
like an echo in a well.

Haystacks climb gentle hills
in single-file, walk over fields,
appear again opposite,
swallowed by a misty flicker.
From above chalky light dust
blurs the dark green shadows.

The people are isolated,
lonely and silent.
Life is borrowed, weighs itself
against the weak present
which spoils fast and decays.
Timelessness is now
overshadowing eternity.

Irish Writers' Groups

As if gathered
around a campfire,
in an adventurously daring way,
in joyful anticipation,
the flickering glow of a fire
on expectant faces.
It seems like a lifetime ago.
How lonely one must get,
to recognize all
what the poetry tree yields,
in its diversity?
Every work a single leaf.
Harvested ripe fruits.
Sharp edges that cast soft shadows,
that make the green blush.
Each leaf with inscription.
Heart-shaped leaves,
beginning of novels,
final lines, reading samples,
long-sought-after rhymes
engraved into pages.
A gift for each of us,
breathed on ethereal paper,
each a unique work of art.
Detached we are,
as if we were an inclusion,
trapped in a drop of amber.
Here, in company, we fly free,
like a liberated bee,
we leave legible traces,
using lost words.

Deliver boldly unheard speeches,
backdate stories,
revitalize deleted words,
steer a sentence around corners.
We keep quiet during the week
on Sundays we speak freely.
The laurel suits a few,
some are admitted into sacred halls.
We uphold our common vow,
of telling each other stories
until the end, impart
ballads if necessary
share literary jewels.
Oh, my friends,
how I miss the promised land of poetry.
In the beginning was the logos,
we are immortal only through the word.

Eduard Schmidt-Zorner

New Family

I leaf through my life's logbook,
that lies worn and dog-eared,
in front of me, opened,
with its yellowed pages,
and I review the time
and decipher the words
and find the term "family"
in different contexts.

'Family' always sounds homely,
consists of three people or more
and can amount to a *clan*.
As an orphan, I no longer have one.
The bonds with cousins
are stretched thin and long.

Soon I called strangers,
(now friends),
brothers and sisters,
accepted them as my new family.
They dug their way into my heart
and never disappointed me.

We now form a tight bond
from many parts of the world.
A colourful kaleidoscope:
Poland, Ireland,
Ukraine, Germany
Uzbekistan, Italy,
UK, USA,
Albania, North Africa,
Kurdistan, Romania.

We are all one family.
They love me, the old man,
and I consider them cousins and kindreds.
'Family' sounds familiar,
the same in almost all languages.

Displaced Language

In the beginning
I had only one language.
Objects, feelings,
colours and dreams,
were enclosed in it
like flies
in a piece of amber.

At the age of four
a second one was added;
imposed,
my father loved the French.
His own experience taught him
to have several tongues
and a handful of passports,
not to run the risk to be
trapped, held hostage
by hostile regimes
as it happened to him once.

Decades ago
I learned my first English words.
Now I write for five years, actively,
but still unable to express myself
as I wished I could, satisfactorily,
not to inflict pain
on the audience.

I do not speak correctly,
bit broken, with an appalling accent,
write by consulting dictionaries,
call the other languages
enemy languages.

The reason,
a serious one:
these languages
are gradually
killing my mother tongue.

You become a writer
by writing patiently, arduously,
without ever losing faith
in what you write.

I write by the light of the moon,
the full moon, in the night,
under the fertile moonlight,
sentences take shape.
They circle around me,
get a rhythm, rhymes,
a melody, become poems.

Memory refuses to recall moments
in which I have lost part of my life.
I lost my ethnicity in a cold January,
a life of strife.
I would have written anywhere
where I would have settled
and in the language of that place.

I did not choose a language.
They came to me by fate,
by chance, by circumstances,
they opened a gate
to other spheres.
To be an emigrant is a challenge,
a wanderer between worlds
and words.

Traces

A stone pushed with the foot.
Wind that tousled the hair.

The sea we walked into.
There was sand and supple grass.

The stone is still there,
the sea comes and goes,
and the grass draws half-moons.

An apple in the hand,
a ball
and a red sun on the horizon.
You hold yourself by the hand.

Listening to the distant sound
It seems so long ago.

Killorglin

I take my way on the road,
south from the *Curragh*,
past *Drom An Bhaile* burial ground,
the mountain range in view
which tells the current weather
better
than a forecast.

Sometimes its slopes are white,
with frost or snow bedight,
then grey on an autumn day,
green-purple, when the heather grows,
sometimes black, draped in clouds,
or sunlit on a summer day.

The peaceful *Laune* river,
as a fluvial border,
its bridge reaches out
to the opposite side,
under which fish glide,
and swans move on.

A church on the horizon,
abandoned, defunct,
today a temple of *Dionysus*,
where was on the top of this mound,
seven hundred years ago,
a Knights Templars' encampment,
and the white cloaks of the knights
stood out against the blue sky
until the French king betrayed them.

Climbing *Lower Bridge Street*
is like a penitential path,
arduous, steep
like the way to *Golgotha*.
By the time you reach the top,
all pain and trouble are gone -
St. James chimes twelve.
A bit of rain runs off the ivy
on the one remaining wall
of *Conway Castle*
where you can raise a pint
to the *FitzGeralds* and *Conways*
in the beer garden of *Kingston's*.

Cheers.
I will meet my poet friends
in the library
to recite this poem to them.

Eduard Schmidt-Zorner

A Storm of Birds

A murder of black crows
darkens the sky,
they caw loud,
ascend, descend,
sinister objects,
which mean danger, a threat,
write dark signs on the clouds,
produce a raucous cry,
let a long black ribbon flutter by.

Now they pass in unison,
the blue expanse unfolds again,
they get smaller on the horizon.

Then with an even louder cry
follows a seagull colony,
like stormy sea surf's breaking waves,
washed to the shore, white crests,
to be absorbed by the blue of the West
and disappear, merge with the mist,
chandelle towards the sea.

A tiding of magpies,
in chessboard fashion,
hovers,
their chatter resounds,
they fly their rounds gently,
watch the field attentively.
It is their habitat,
a field full of rushes,
surrounded by blackthorn bushes.

They reign over those acres.
The black and white armies
were only passing through.

A chaffinch without its flock,
unimpressed by the commotion,
though cautious, perches on a rock,
tilts its head, eyes a beetle,
and flies on, chirping,
into the shelter of the shrubs.

Peace and quiet again.

Ode to the Couple

In a kind of paradise,
full of meadow fields,
near floodplain forests,
they have met.
Ethereal the slopes,
rocky, craggy, wildly jagged,
steep paths, wide green expanse,
they found each other.

Siobhán,
from the gentle valley
of *Gleann Ó Ruachta* barony
where the *Roughty* River flows
into the *Kenmare* Bay
where the mountain range
of *Barr Éirnín*
towers above *Cill Gharbháin*
where the Normans were defeated
in the *Battle of Callann*

and

Eoghan,
he comes from the wide fields,
the green mild wavy pastures,
an unobstructed view of the mountains,
to the west
where the sun sinks in the Atlantic Ocean.
unobstructed as his mind and gaze
himself serene, matter of fact,
strong as the Reeks.

An old poet like me
may give some advice:
life is not easy,
the burdens might increase,
the way sometimes becomes stony,
but two shoulders carry half the load,
understanding makes the burden lighter,
smiling can reduce its weight,
Always forgive and forget,
let a jade rainbow span a bow
after rain. Over your mutual way.

Today we experienced a ray of hope,
hope in the darkness,
in this darkening time.

You have tied the knot.
This is a victory over doom,
A good omen.
A victory of tenacity,
perseverance and maturity.

A sign of the power of light
was the sun, the clear weather
that lay over *Kilgarvan*
and the mountains,
as strong, as powerful,
as endless and manifest,
that is what we wish you both
to be your life together.

You are light-bringers,
bringing hope and kindness
into our time, to our place,
to parents, brothers, and sisters,
relatives, neighbours, and friends.
A good sign. A promise.

Our good wishes are with you
always
on your sunlit path.

Poetry Along the River Laune

Over lush pastureland tower
the *Reeks*
not near enough
to reflect in the flowing water
of the silently moving river,
that copies the sky,
once blue, then grey,
sometimes menacing black
when constant rain causes
rising water
to lick over the roads
and cover the plain
near *Ballymalis* Castle.

The Greeks know the word *eleutheria*
'To go where you want to go"
(to elthein opou erá)
That is freedom.
So free as our 'kingdom' surrounded by seas,
guarded by elves under sacred trees.
They worship a ram as they worshipped *Pan*,
the god of nature and rustic men,
never a temple dedicated to him,
so free and independent as he was,
as were the shepherds and hunters
of the *Laune* valley.

At his time there must have grown
elm trees along his banks
because in *Cois Leamhán*
elm tree is in its name.
Beside the elm, the sacred tree,
for druids the divine feminine,
the elm offers hope of revival
and rebirth, rich harvest
and hay saving
to follow the farmers' saying:
"When the elm leaf
is as big as a mouse's ear,
then sow barley never fear"

A *puck* goat is made king
for three days,
reminds us of *Cernunnos*,
from the Celtic gods' pantheon,
the god of beasts and wild places,
a bearded man with antlers,
a mediator of man and nature,
able to tame prey and predator,
so, they might lie down together.

In this place is mysticism,
all interwoven:
From the Knights Templars
who cherished the elm,
who would add "...of the elm"
at the end of their church's name
to a hidden chapel near the river,
said to contain a face,
Baphomet,
the goat-like mystic figure,
and a stone with a triple cross
in Ardmoneel,
the sign of a templar's preceptor
near this *Laune* river
which empties into the wide sea.

Glossary

Cead Mile Failte - a hundred thousand welcomes
Glen – Valley
Conas atá tú, ar maidin? - How are you this morning?
Tá an gruaighe go háilinn - The hair is beautiful.
Grand Parade - one of the main streets of Cork city, Ireland.
Venice Éireann - Irish Venice.
Crubeens - (from Irish crúibín, meaning "pig's trotter") an Irish dish made of boiled pigs' feet.
Drisheen - (Irish: drisín) a type of blood pudding made in Ireland.
St. Augustine's Church - a Roman Catholic Church belonging to the Augustinian Order located on Washington Street in Cork City.
Tuckey Street - home of the Provincial Grand Lodge
St. Anne Shandon, Cork - one of the oldest churches in the city built in 1722 noted for its eight bells, immortalised in the song *The Bells of Shandon* by Francis Sylvester
Sneem - (Irish: An tSnaidhm) a village situated on the Iveragh Peninsula in County Kerry, in the southwest of Ireland.
Cosan na Naomh - Saints'Road, 18 kilometer Pilgrim Path in County Kerry in South-West Ireland.
Ard-na-Sidhe - Hill of the Fairies
Butler's Arms - Hotel in Waterville
Doonreaghan - Place in Kerry, with beautiful landscape.
Skelligs - Islands (Irish: Na Scealaga) two small, steep, and rocky islands lying about 13 kilometers (8 miles) west of Bolus Head on the Iveragh Peninsula in County Kerry, Ireland.
Taoisech - Irish for Prime Minister

An Cromán - Cromane is a fishers' village located in County Kerry, Ireland.

Kenmare - (Irish: Neidín, meaning 'the little nest') a small town in the south of County Kerry, Ireland. The name Kenmare is the anglicised form of *Ceann Mara*, meaning "head of the sea", referring to the head of Kenmare Bay.

Iveragh Peninsula - (Irish: Uíbh Ráthach) located in County Kerry in Ireland. It is the largest peninsula in southwestern Ireland. A mountain range, the MacGillycuddy's Reeks, lies in the centre of the peninsula.

Puck - (Irish: Aonach an Phoic, meaning "Fair of the He-Goat", 'poc' being the Irish for a male goat) one of Ireland's oldest fairs. It takes place annually from 10–12 August in Killorglin, County Kerry.

Dromavally - Graveyard between Milltown and Killorglin

Fenit - Deep Sea Port near Tralee

Bolteens - Village on the Dingle Peninsula

Fuil Cheilteach - Celtic Blood

Máthair - Mother

Sleán - spade for cutting turf

Torc - a large rigid or stiff neck ring in metal

Gallia est omnis divisa in partes tres... - All Gaul is divided into three parts- Caesar "Gallic War"

Andraste - an Icenic war goddess invoked by Boudica in her fight against the Roman occupation of Britain in AD 60.

Callanafersy - 3.3 kilometers (2.1 miles) north of Killorglin

Milltown - home town of the poet who wrote these poems

Castlemaine - near Milltown

Tralee - Bigger town on the other side of the Mangerton mountains

Tuath(a) Dé Danann - a supernatural race in Irish mythology. Many of them are thought to represent deities of pre-Christian Gaelic Ireland.

Scotia - A short distance from the bustling Irish town of Tralee in County Kerry there is an otherworldly looking glen which is known as *Scotia's Grave*. According to Irish folklore, the glen was the location of a battle which took place between the Celtic Milesians and the Tuatha Dé Danann.

Tinnahally - townland near Milltown

MacGillycuddy's Reeks - mountain range in the middle of the Iverah Peninsula

Crann Bethadh - Tree of Life

Eire - Ireland

Uisneach - described as the sacred centre of Ireland.

Dóchas - Hope

Listowel - town in North Kerry. The "Literary Capital of Ireland", a number of internationally known playwrights and authors have lived there, including Bryan MacMahon and John B. Keane.

Seanchai - Irish storyteller, now the name of the Writers' Museum in Listowel. Means: Bearer of old lore.

Siobhán - a female given name of Irish origin.

Gleann Ó Ruachta / Glanarought - Valley of the Roughty River, near Kilgarvan

Roughty River - flows into the Kenmare Bay

Barr Éirnín - Barrerneen mountain or mountain range

Cill Gharbháin - Kilgarvan, meaning 'Garvan's church') is a small village in County Kerry, Ireland. It is situated on the banks of the Roughty River which flows into Kenmare Bay.

Battle of Callann – Battle fought in August 1261 between the Hiberno-Normans, under John FitzGerald, and three Gaelic clans: MacCarthy, who held the Kingdom of Desmond, under Fínghin Mac Carthaigh, King of Desmond, ancestor of the MacCarthy Reagh dynasty. It took place in the townland of Callann or Collo near modern-day Kilgarvan, County Kerry. Result: Gaelic victory, total annihilation of adventuring English army

Eoghan - an early Irish male name
Curragh - a hill near Killorglin
Drom An Bhaile - burial ground near Killorglin
Killorglin - in the geographical heart of County Kerry, is home to Ireland's oldest fair.
Laune - river flows through Killorglin
Conway Castle - Castle Conway is a former castle and stately home in the town of Killorglin, County Kerry, Ireland. Today only the ruins of one wall remain **in the beer garden of**
Kingston's - Originally called Killorglin Castle, a defensive structure was first built on the site next to the River Laune by Maurice FitzGerald, 2nd Lord of Offaly.
Ballymalis - Castle is a tower house and National Monument located between Killarney and Killorglin, Co. Kerry
Cois Leamhán - beside the elms
Cernunnos - a horned god found in Celtic mythology. Celtic god of the forest.
Baphomet - a symbol of balance in various occult and mystical traditions, associated with the Gnostics and Templars, although occasionally purported to be a deity or a demon.
Ardmoneel - townland near Killorglin.

About the Poet

Photograph by Heinz-Ullrich **Isselbächer**.
Tannenweg 33. 35687 Dillenburg-Niederscheld.
www.issel-photo.com

Eduard Schmidt-Zorner is a translator and writer of poetry, haibun, haiku and short stories. He writes in four languages: English, French, Spanish, and German. He also writes under his pen name: Eadbhard McGowan.

He is a member of four writer groups in Ireland and has lived in County Kerry, Ireland, for more than 30 years and is a proud Irish citizen, born in Germany.

He is published in over 200 anthologies, literary journals and broadsheets in the USA, UK, Ireland, Australia, Canada, Japan, Sweden, Spain, Italy, France, Austria, Bangladesh, India, Mauritius, Nepal, Nigeria, Nepal, and Pakistan.

www.ingramcontent.com/pod-product-compliance
Lightning Source LLC
Chambersburg PA
CBHW061749020426
42331CB00006B/1408